AI INNOVATIONS

HOW TECHNOLOGY IS PUSHING THE BOUNDARIES

Understanding and Using Artificial Intelligence: An AI Book

Jhon Dujardin

Imprint

Publisher:
John Dujardin
SDCJAK CO., LTD
3/7 Sukhumvit Soi 18, 10110 Bangkok, Thailand
info@thaipan-legal.com

We have carefully researched and checked all the information in this book. Nevertheless, the publisher and the author assume no liability for damage or disadvantages that may arise from the use of the information contained in this book.

Although the book has been carefully edited, errors can still creep in. We thank you in advance for your comments and are grateful for every suggestion for improvement.

FOREWORD

Hello you! I am glad that you have chosen the book about artificial intelligence (AI). As a valued reader of this book, I would like to address you directly. At a time when technology and data play an increasingly important role in our daily lives, it is of great importance to be informed about the possibilities and challenges of AI.

The motivation behind this book is based on my personal interest and experience with artificial intelligence. After using AI for the first time, I was very excited about this technology. It will fundamentally change the economy in the future and new jobs will be created while others will disappear. These changes can already be observed in many sectors. AI makes it possible to work faster, more cost-effectively, and often better than human professionals. I, too, now generate a large part of my income through a wide variety of applications of artificial intelligence.

You must be aware of the possibilities and effects of AI to use them for you. A refusal or ignorance of this technology can mean disadvantages for many people. However, as with any new technology, it's also important to maintain a healthy dose of skepticism.

The aim of this book is to present the opportunities and challenges of AI and to reduce fears of this new technology. We will give an introduction to the world of AI and explain what AI is, how it works and what applications already exist. We will also discuss how AI will change your life and work.

This book is of interest to anyone interested in technology, the future, and societal changes, whether you are a student, a professional, or just curious. You will find a lot of interesting information in this book.

For reasons of readability and to simplify the wording, gender-appropriate language is not used. However, all individuals are addressed equally.

TABLE OF CONTENTS

4. HUMAN RESPONSIBILITY IN THE ERA OF ARTIFICIAL INTELLIGENCE: A DISCUSSION ON CHALLENGES AND SOLUTIONS

THE MOST POWERFUL AI TOOLS AT A GLANCE

copy.ai

chatgpt.com

pictory.com

mangools.com

AI DEMYSTIFIED:
Foundations and applications of artificial intelligence

Welcome to an exciting journey into the fascinating world of artificial intelligence (AI). Recently, AI has experienced rapid development and has grown from an abstract idea to a practical application. AI systems are ubiquitous these days, from voice assistants like Siri and Alexa to self-driving cars and modern medical diagnostic systems.

Artificial intelligence has the potential to improve our lives on various levels and to change our everyday work, our learning behavior and our entertainment in the long term. At the same time, there are also concerns that AI could jeopardize jobs and influence societal power structures.

This book offers you a detailed introduction to the fascinating world of artificial intelligence (AI). Together, we will examine how AI came about what possibilities it offers today and how it could be used in the future. You will learn about the different types of AI systems and how they are used in different fields like business, healthcare, education, and many others. We will also look at the history of AI, from its beginnings in the 1950s to the latest developments and technologies. In addition to the benefits of AI, we will also address challenges such as privacy and ethics. I will also show you how you can use AI to your advantage and what the possible risks are. I invite you to join me on an exciting journey through the world of AI and how it will affect our lives.

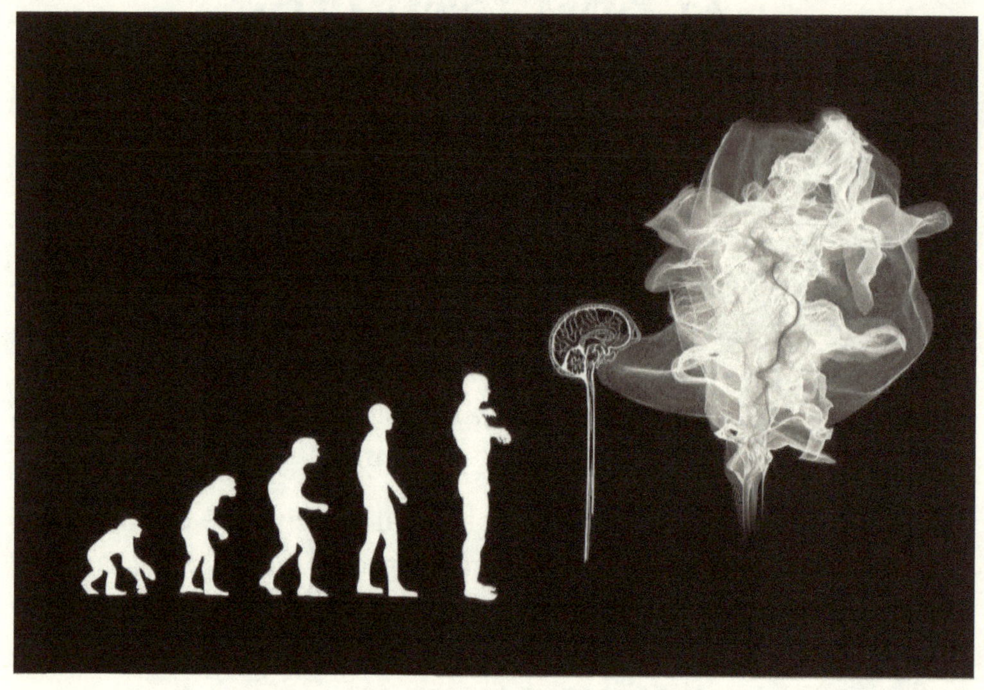

Source: https://pixabay.com

(1)

AI – BEHIND THE SCENES:
What we should know about the technology

In this chapter, you will get a comprehensive introduction to the exciting world of artificial intelligence. We will look at the history and current developments in this field and provide an overview of which companies and organizations play an important role in the AI industry. Furthermore, we will deal with an important question: does the proliferation of AI have an impact on the capitalist system and if so, which ones? So let's dive together into the fascinating world of AI and also discuss critical questions.

1.1 THE FUTURE OF THINKING: AN INTRODUCTION TO ARTIFICIAL INTELLIGENCE

In general, it can be said that artificial intelligence (AI) is a subfield of computer science that deals with the development of systems and programs that can imitate human-like intelligence. In particular, this involves the ability to solve complex problems, make decisions and automate processes.

Various techniques and methods are usually used, such as machine learning, neural networks or expert systems. The aim is to train the machine in such a way that it can perform certain tasks independently and effectively without having to rely on explicit programming or human help.

The areas of application of AI are very diverse and range from image and speech recognition to robotics to automated data analysis and process optimization in companies. In particular, the focus is on improving efficiency, accuracy, and speed.

There are already numerous areas of application for AI systems in our daily lives. These are often used in places where you don't necessarily expect them. For example, with voice recognition on our smartphones, with recommendations on streaming platforms, or with the monitoring of financial markets.

It is therefore worth taking a closer look and realizing that AI systems can play a role in many everyday situations. Maybe the next application of AI is even in your pocket, and you use it every day without even realizing it.

1.2 The Evolution of Artificial Thinking: A Journey Through the Centuries

The history of the emergence of artificial intelligence is a long journey through the centuries, which has its origins in philosophy and mathematics. Over the past few decades, the modern form of AI has evolved as computer scientists and mathematicians began to explore the possibility of computer-based intelligence.

An early pioneer in this field was John McCarthy, a computer scientist at Stanford University, who coined the term "artificial intelligence," laying the foundation for modern research in the field. Over time, numerous other scientists and researchers around the world have contributed to the development of AI and in doing so, have written a fascinating story.

The recently deceased computer scientist is widely regarded as the "father of AI". He was instrumental in introducing modern AI research and has led numerous conferences and workshops in this field.

In the 1960s and 1970s, researchers under his leadership developed the first artificial intelligence systems that form the basis for today's developments. The "ELIZA" program, which demonstrated a simple form of natural language processing and was thus groundbreaking for many later developments, is particularly well known.

During the early development of AI, the first expert systems capable of performing specific tasks in a limited context were developed. Expectations for the possibilities of AI were high and it was expected that in the near future computers would develop human-like intelligence and solve many problems that are difficult or even impossible for humans to solve.

However, many of those early expectations turned out to be overly optimistic, and there was a decline in interest in AI in the 1970s and 1980s, dubbed the "AI winter." This was mainly because the technology was not yet advanced enough to deliver on many of the promises it made in the early days.

Then, in the 1980s and 1990s, there was a boom in AI research focused on the use of AI in practice. Companies like IBM and Microsoft have invested heavily in research and development of AI technologies, and there have been many significant advances in areas such as machine learning, artificial neural networks, and pattern recognition.

This fact has contributed to a renaissance in AI over the past few decades, and it has led to a variety of applications in areas such as speech processing, image recognition, and recommender systems. AI research has seen a tremendous upswing lately, and this trend is expected to continue as technology advances.

1.3 Artificial intelligence in practice: an inventory

In recent decades, the rapid development of AI has resulted in more advanced and powerful technology capable of performing human-like tasks. Accessibility to big data and powerful computing systems has enabled researchers and developers to train complex AI systems capable of automating processes, performing data analysis and making forecasts.

However, the legitimate question arises as to who will benefit from this development. While there are many benefits to using AI technology, those benefits can be unevenly distributed. Those who have access to resources and expertise to develop and use AI systems can benefit from this technology by increasing their efficiency and improving their business processes.

On the other hand, workers in industries affected by automation may lose their jobs or their working conditions may deteriorate. Additionally, unequal access to AI technology can put some people or companies ahead of others, resulting in a competitive advantage.

We must be aware of who will benefit from the development of AI and who may be disadvantaged. It is also important to consider the impact of AI on the world of work and society in general, and take steps to ensure that the benefits of AI technology are accessible to all and that no one is left behind.

1.4 AI Giants: The companies that dominate the industry

It is crucial that artificial intelligence be beneficial to society as a whole and that everyone can benefit from it. The leading companies and organizations in the AI industry play an important role in creating progress and innovation that is accessible to the public. Big players in the AI industry include Google with its research department Google AI and AI tools like Google Assistant and Google Translate, Microsoft with its advanced AI tools and solutions like Microsoft Azure and Cortana, Amazon with its AI-powered products such as Amazon Alexa and Amazon Recognition, IBM with a long history in the AI industry and a range of AI tools and solutions including IBM Watson, and OpenAI, a research-oriented company recognized for its work in machine learning and the deep learning is known. ChatGPT is a language model developed by OpenAI and is now used for many applications. It is important that AI development be accessible and beneficial to all to ensure fair and equitable use.

If you are interested in ChatGPT or how to monetize the model, check out the ChatGPT Bible. The book is available free of charge and shows various detailed ways to earn money with the program, almost completely automatically.

"The AI Bible, making money with artificial intelligence: Real case studies and instructions for implementation."

In my view, the companies mentioned above have a great influence on AI development and the spread of AI solutions worldwide. However, it is also important to emphasize that AI technology should not only benefit large companies, but should also be used by small businesses and individuals to create innovative solutions and let society as a whole benefit from them. It is crucial that the benefits of AI technology are shared fairly and that no one is left out. It is the responsibility of governments and companies to ensure that AI development is used for of all and does not have a negative impact on society.

1.5 AI and the Concentration of Wealth: Who Benefits from the AI Revolution?

There are numerous debates about the extent to which AI threatens capitalism. Some experts argue that AI can help optimize existing economic processes and business models and strengthen capitalism by helping companies operate more efficiently and profitably. Others, however, see the danger that AI will lead to corporate dominance and displace human jobs and reduce human income, which eventually could endanger the fundamental principles of capitalism.

There is also concern that AI could bring about a shift in the way value is created, and that new economic models are needed to capture this shift. However, the exact impact of AI on capitalism is still uncertain and depends on a variety of factors including regulation, job availability and income distribution. It is therefore of great importance that governments, companies, and society are actively involved in shaping the future use of AI to minimize negative impacts and maximize positive ones.

A basic introduction to the topic of artificial intelligence (AI) was given on the last few pages, including a definition and a historical overview of its development. It was also emphasized that AI is now playing an increasingly important role in all walks of life and is being pushed by big companies like Google, Amazon, and Facebook. In addition, the challenge of AI for capitalism was addressed.

(2)

THE MAIN AI SYSTEMS:

An overview of their functions and applications

This chapter is about the different types of AI systems that rely on different technologies and methods to accomplish different tasks. As John Giannandrea, senior vice president of AI and machine learning at Google, points out, artificial intelligence will not only change the way we work, but also how we must think to be successful. Therefore, it is important to develop an understanding of the different types of AI systems to better assess their impact on our lives and work.

2.1 <u>Machine Learning: Understanding the Basics</u>

This section introduces the three main types of machine learning: unsupervised learning, supervised learning, and deep learning. Each of these types uses different technologies and methods to learn from data and make predictions. In unsupervised learning, the system automatically recognizes patterns and structures in large amounts of data without being given specific goals or categories. An example of unsupervised learning is the clustering technique, in which data is automatically divided into different groups. In contrast, in supervised learning, the system is trained by human supervisors, who provide it with sample data and provide the correct answers. This mainly solves categorization problems. Finally, there is deep learning, which is a specialized form of supervised learning and is primarily used for complex tasks such as speech recognition or image processing.

Deep Learning

It is a special form of machine learning based on neural networks. It allows computer systems to recognize very complex patterns in data and make predictions by using multiple layers of neurons. An example of deep learning is using AI to recognize and identify faces in photos. In general, machine learning has many applications across all industries, such as finance, healthcare, defense, marketing, and retail. It can be used to automate business processes, improve customer care, predict markets and trends, and develop personalized products and services.

Deep Neural Networks

Neural networks are an important part of machine learning and are based on the concept of the human brain. They are programmed to analyze data and recognize patterns using layers of artificial neurons that are connected. Neural networks find applications in various fields, such as language translation, image classification, and predicting financial trends. A well-known example of the use of neural networks is "computer vision", in which a system can recognize and categorize images by analyzing characteristics such as colors, shapes, and structures. Neural networks are also crucial for autonomous driving because of their ability to recognize and process complex patterns in the vehicle's sensor data, which can come from various sources such as cameras, radar, LIDAR and GPS.

The neural network is programmed through training to learn various driving tasks, such as lane keeping, cruise control, obstacle avoidance, and road sign recognition. By applying machine learning techniques, the neural network can be continuously improved and optimized to optimally fulfill the driving task and ensure maximum safety.

Another example of the use of neural networks is medical diagnostics. Here, systems use images of diseases and health, such. X-rays and MRIs, trained to recognize patterns and make a diagnosis.

It is important to note that neural networks are not perfect, and there remain many challenges that need to be solved to improve the efficiency and accuracy of these systems. Still, neural networks have huge potential and are an active area of research within the AI community.

Rule-based AI systems

Rule-based AI systems, also known as "expert systems", are a special type of artificial intelligence based on fixed rules and processes. These rules and processes are defined by humans and taught to the system to solve specific problems. In contrast, supervised learning is based on a machine learning approach, in which the algorithm uses training data to learn how to solve a specific problem. Rule-based AI systems use decision trees and a set of rules to solve problems. An example of a rule-based AI system is a medical diagnostic system that makes a diagnosis based on symptoms, risk factors, and medical histories. It uses a set of rules developed by doctors and experts to determine which diagnoses to diagnose based on the data at hand. Another example is a customer service chatbot that works on a fixed rule basis. The chatbot can answer customers' questions and help them with problems using a set of rules and processes defined by customer service professionals. Rule-based AI systems are very reliable and accurate because they work on a fixed rule base and are easier to implement and monitor than other types of AI systems, such as neural networks. However, it should be noted that rule-based AI systems are limited, as they can only solve problems for which clear rules and processes have been defined. If an issue arises that is not covered by the existing rules, the system will not be able to find a solution.

2.2 <u>Evolutionary Algorithms</u>

There are alternative approaches to rule-based AI systems, such as neural networks, genetic algorithms, and unsupervised learning. Neural networks can recognize complex patterns in data and learn independently by adjusting weights and connections between the artificial neurons. Genetic algorithms are based on principles of evolution and adapt through mutation and selection processes to find an optimal solution. Unsupervised learning is an approach where the system has no predefined rules or labels and can learn from exploring patterns in the data itself. These alternative approaches can be used in various application areas such as image recognition, speech recognition and decision-making.

In addition, rule-based AI systems must contain expert-defined rules and processes that make it difficult to quickly adapt to changes and new circumstances. This makes them less flexible than other AI systems, such as neural networks, which can learn from data and adapt themselves. Furthermore, due to their limited ability to understand context, rule-based AI systems can struggle to solve complex problems where there are many variables and unknowns.

In the previous chapter, you were introduced to the main AI systems and some applications, including expert systems, neural networks, and machine learning. By understanding these different AI systems and applications, you can understand the many possibilities that AI offers you.

(3)

APPLICATION AREAS OF ARTIFICIAL INTELLIGENCE

As you have certainly noticed, artificial intelligence has made enormous progress recently and has already fundamentally changed numerous areas of our lives. Whether process automation, data analysis or knowledge generation – the possible uses of AI are almost limitless.

For example, in the healthcare industry, AI is used to diagnose and treat diseases, while in the financial industry, it helps predict markets and risks. Art and entertainment are also using AI to create new pieces of music and films, while in traffic engineering it is helping to prevent accidents and optimize traffic flow.

In addition, AI has the potential to make a major contribution to improving living conditions in developing countries, for example by monitoring environmental conditions, fighting diseases and improving education.

It remains exciting to see how AI will open up more and more areas of application in the future and improve the everyday lives of billions of people. In the following sections, specific fields of application of AI are presented.

3.1) <u>Medicine</u>

From diagnosing diseases to discovering new medicines, AI has already found numerous applications in medicine.

One area where AI is particularly useful is in diagnosing diseases. AI systems can analyze large amounts of data and recognize patterns that are difficult for human doctors to detect. For example, an AI system can use CT scans or X-rays to automatically detect abnormalities such as tumors or injuries, which can help doctors diagnose and treat diseases. Another example is the use of AI for the early detection of Alzheimer's. AI systems can detect signals associated with the disease before they show overt symptoms in patients.

In addition to diagnosis, AI can also help in the development of new medicines. Traditional drug development can take years and often costs hundreds of millions of dollars. However, AI systems can speed up the search for potential drugs by analyzing large amounts of data to identify compounds that might be useful in treating diseases. Some companies have already used AI systems to develop new drugs and speed up the clinical trial process.

Another area where AI is being used in medicine is in personalized medicine. By analyzing data such as genetic information, medical images and other clinical data, AI can help tailor treatments to patients. This allows physicians to create treatment plans tailored to the patient's specific needs and risk factors. AI systems can also improve disease prediction by combining data from different sources to identify risk factors and make accurate predictions.

However, there are also some challenges when using AI in medicine. One of the biggest is the security of patient data.

Since AI systems have to analyze large amounts of data, there is a risk that sensitive information will be disclosed. It is therefore important to ensure that data is anonymized and that strict security measures are in place to ensure the confidentiality of patient data.

Another problem is the need to adapt AI systems to clinical environments. Most AI systems are developed and tested in laboratory environments, and it is often difficult to integrate them into the real conditions of clinics and hospitals. Another field of application for AI in medicine is personalized medicine. Here, data from patients such as genome sequencing, clinical data and other factors are analyzed to create individual treatment plans. By leveraging AI, doctors and researchers can more quickly and accurately make predictions about the effectiveness of certain treatments and predict potential side effects.

An example of the use of AI in personalized medicine is cancer treatment. By analyzing genomic data of the tumor and the patient, AI systems can create individual treatment plans tailored to the specific genetic characteristics of the tumor and the patient. This can help patients receive more effective treatments and minimize side effects.

Another field of application is diagnostics. AI systems can make precise diagnoses and enable fast and effective treatment. For example, AI systems can identify and classify certain diseases or abnormalities based on pattern recognition on X-rays, CT scans or MRI images.

However, there are also challenges related to the use of AI in medicine. One of the most immense challenges is the security and confidentiality of patient data. AI systems require large amounts of data to function effectively, and it is important to ensure that this data is protected, and patient privacy is maintained.

Another problem is the misinterpretation of data by AI systems. When under trained or misused, AI systems can make inaccurate predictions or misdiagnoses, which can lead to inappropriate treatments.

Despite these challenges, the use of AI in medicine has the potential to transform the way diseases are diagnosed and treated. The integration of AI systems into medical practice is expected to continue to increase in the coming years, helping to improve patient health and well-being.

3.2) <u>Finance</u>

Artificial intelligence has made great strides in the financial industry lately and is now used in many areas, from lending to fraud detection to predicting markets and risks.

One of the most important applications of AI in the financial industry is data analysis. AI algorithms can quickly and effectively analyze large amounts of data to identify trends and patterns. In this way, financial institutions can, for example, better assess credit risks and make predictions about the future development of markets and asset classes.

Another important area is fraud detection. AI can help identify fraudulent activity by monitoring data for unusual patterns. This enables financial institutions to react more quickly to possible cases of fraud and better protect their customers.

Around customer care, AI-supported chatbots and virtual assistants can be used to answer customer inquiries quickly and efficiently. This can help increase customer satisfaction while reducing customer support costs.

Another field of application of AI in the financial industry is the prediction of markets and risks. AI algorithms can analyze historical data and identify trends to make predictions about how markets and asset classes will perform in the future. This can benefit financial institutions' investment decisions and help them better diversify their portfolio.

Despite the many benefits that AI applications offer in the financial industry, there are also safety and ethical concerns. For example, AI algorithms could make inaccurate predictions or even promote discrimination due to faulty data or biases.

It is therefore important that financial institutions exercise due diligence when implementing AI systems and ensure that the systems are fair and transparent. You should also ensure that the systems are adequately protected against external attacks.

Overall, the application of AI in the financial industry offers many advantages, from risk assessment to customer care. However, it is important that financial institutions exercise due diligence and ensure their systems are fair, transparent, and secure.

3.3) Mobility

The possibilities that AI offers are almost unlimited in this area. In this article, we will take a closer look at the different applications of AI in mobility.

Traffic monitoring and optimization One of the main applications of AI in mobility is traffic monitoring and optimization. Through the use of sensors and cameras, road surveillance systems can automatically record and analyze traffic flows and, based on this, control traffic signals and traffic lights to optimize traffic. AI-based algorithms can also predict traffic patterns, thus preventing traffic jams and accidents.

Autonomous Vehicles AI is also an important part of autonomous vehicles. AI algorithms enable autonomous vehicles to collect and interpret data from various sensors to make real-time decisions. These decisions can include everything from vehicle speed and direction to navigation and obstacle avoidance.

Customer service and personalization AI can also be used in the mobility industry to improve customer service and offer personalized services. Chatbots and voice assistants can answer customer questions and help book rides. AI can also be used to analyze customers' driving habits and provide personalized offers and recommendations.

Maintenance and repair AI can also be used in the maintenance and repair of vehicles. By monitoring sensors and data from the vehicle, AI algorithms can identify problems early and recommend preventive maintenance actions. This minimizes downtime and reduces costs.

Security is another area where AI is being used in the mobility industry. AI-based algorithms can recognize and predict driver and pedestrian behavior to avoid accidents. AI can also help in detecting fraud in the proponents arguing that AI-based mobility solutions are safer, more efficient and greener. Opponents fear AI-based vehicles could destroy jobs and pose privacy issues.

Source: pixabay.com

3.4) <u>Education Industry</u>

The education industry is no exception and has started exploring the possibilities of AI applications to improve the way we learn, teach and expand our knowledge.

One of the greatest challenges in education is personalizing learning to meet the diverse needs and abilities of each student. AI can help here by collecting and analyzing data about a student's learning behavior to recommend personalized learning content and methods. This can help give students a more profound understanding of the topics and improve their learning performance.

Another way AI can be used in education is to automatically score tests and exams. Instead of teachers having to spend hours completing paperwork, AI algorithms can quickly and efficiently score student responses and provide feedback. This not only saves time, but also helps minimize human error and bias in the assessment.

Furthermore, AI can also be used in the development of learning content. AI-based chatbots can provide students with interactive learning opportunities and respond to their questions and concerns to give them a more profound understanding of the materials. Likewise, AI-powered learning programs can customize and improve content by collecting and analyzing student feedback to optimize its effectiveness.

Finally, AI can also be used to support teachers. AI-powered curriculum planning can help teachers create and organize effective learning content, while AI-powered analytics tools can help teachers monitor and understand their students' progress and performance.

While there are still challenges, such as privacy and ethics concerns, the use of AI in education shows tremendous potential for improving learning and teaching. It is expected that the use of AI applications in education will continue to grow in the coming years and become an integral part of the educational experience.

3.5) Speech Recognition and Processing

Thanks to AI technologies, speech data can be analyzed and processed to create machine-generated text and speech output. Applying AI to speech recognition and processing has numerous benefits, from automating speech services to improving accessibility and developing voice assistants.

One of the main applications of AI in speech recognition and processing is the development of voice assistants such as Apple Siri, Amazon Alexa and Google Assistant. These virtual assistants use advanced speech recognition and processing technologies to interpret and respond to user queries. The technologies used in these applications are very advanced, using machine learning and neural networks to recognize and interpret natural language.

Another example of the application of AI in speech recognition and processing is the automatic transcription of speech recordings. AI-based systems can convert audio files into written text, making manual transcription of audio files obsolete. This is particularly useful for transcribing an interview, meeting, lecture or podcast.

Likewise, AI in speech recognition and processing can also help to overcome language barriers and improve barrier-free access to information. AI-based translation programs can translate speaking people in different languages in real time, facilitating communication and information exchange across language and cultural borders.

Additionally, the application of AI in speech recognition and processing can also help in the creation of subtitles for video content. AI-based systems can recognize speech in real time and create subtitles automatically, which is a significant relief, especially for people with hearing disabilities.

Overall, the application of AI in speech recognition and processing offers enormous potential for improving communication and information exchange. While the technology still has challenges and limitations, it is undeniable that AI-based systems are becoming increasingly important for creating accessibility and for automating voice services.

3.6) <u>Image and Face Recognition</u>

The technology has numerous applications in various fields, including security, facial recognition, healthcare, retail and many more.

In the security industry, the use of AI in facial recognition is particularly relevant. AI-based systems can recognize and identify people's faces in a crowd in real time. The technology can also be used in law enforcement to identify criminals based on surveillance footage. Applying AI to facial recognition can also help identify missing persons and thus help save lives.

In medicine, the application of AI in facial recognition can help identify diseases. The technology can recognize facial features that indicate certain diseases, helping to provide faster diagnoses and more effective treatment. AI-based systems can also help identify patients with genetic disorders or those at increased risk of certain diseases.

In the retail industry, applying AI to image recognition can help improve the customer experience. AI-based systems can identify customers through facial recognition and make personalized offers and recommendations. The technology can also be used to monitor shoplifting. While there are numerous benefits to applying AI in image and facial recognition, there are also privacy and ethical concerns. The use of facial recognition can affect the right to privacy and lead to discrimination. The technology is also prone to misidentification and can lead to false arrests.

Overall, the application of AI in image and face recognition offers enormous potential to increase security, improve the customer experience and optimize medical diagnostics. However, it is important that privacy and ethics are considered when using this technology.

Source: pixabay.com

3.8) <u>Production</u>

The technology offers numerous advantages, including higher efficiency, faster production and better quality assurance.

An example of the application of AI in production is predictive maintenance. AI-based systems can use sensors to monitor the health of machines and detect anomalies that indicate future failures. This allows maintenance work to be planned and unforeseen downtime avoided.

Another example is robotics. AI-based systems can program robots to perform complex tasks that humans cannot handle alone. The technology can also be used to streamline production processes by programming robots to perform certain steps faster or more accurately.

Applying AI to production can also help improve quality. AI-based systems can use sensors to monitor quality parameters such as product size, color, or weight. This allows errors to be detected and corrected in real time before defective products go on sale.

Likewise, the application of AI in production can help to reduce waste. AI-based systems can optimize production so that materials are used more effectively and unnecessary waste is avoided.

While there are numerous benefits to using AI in production, there are also challenges. One challenge is that the technology can be expensive, especially for small and medium-sized businesses. Another challenge is that the introduction of AI-based systems in production requires a new type of know-how and skills.

Overall, the use of AI in production offers enormous potential for more efficient production, higher quality assurance and a reduction in waste. However, it is important that companies carefully consider whether and how they can integrate this technology into their production processes.

3.9) <u>Agriculture</u>

The application of artificial intelligence (AI) in agriculture has the potential to improve the efficiency and sustainability of production. The technology can help reduce problems such as yield losses, wasted resources and environmental pollution.

The application of artificial intelligence (AI) in agriculture has the potential to improve the efficiency and sustainability of production. The technology can help reduce problems such as yield losses, wasted resources and environmental pollution.

An example of the application of AI in agriculture is precision farming technology. This technology uses sensors, drones, and other IoT devices to collect data on soil conditions, weather, and plant growth. The data is then analyzed by AI-based systems to make more accurate decisions about irrigation, fertilization, and pest control. As a result, the efficiency of production can be improved by using resources in a more targeted and effective manner.

Another example is the application of AI in animal husbandry. AI-based systems can help monitor animal health by monitoring biological cues such as body weight, exercise, and feed intake. In this way, anomalies can be detected early to enable targeted treatment. In addition, AI-based systems can help improve breeding efficiency by identifying animals with the best genetic traits.

The application of AI in agriculture can also help to reduce environmental pollution. For example, AI-based systems can be used to optimize the use of pesticides and thus reduce consumption. In addition, the technology can help reduce the amount of fertilizer entering the environment, thus contributing to the pollution of water and soil resources.

While the benefits of using AI in agriculture are numerous, there are also challenges. One challenge is that the technology can be expensive, especially for smaller farms. Another challenge is that the introduction of AI-based systems in agriculture requires a new type of know-how and skills.

Overall, the application of AI in agriculture offers enormous potential for more efficient production, higher quality assurance and a reduction in environmental pollution. However, it is important that farmers carefully consider whether and how they can integrate this technology into their production processes.

3.10) <u>Media design</u>

In today's digital world, media creation has become an important part of our daily lives. Whether it's creating graphics, producing videos, or developing websites, media design is a creative process that takes time and resources. However, with advances in artificial intelligence (AI), the way we do media design has changed.

AI systems can be used in many areas of media design. An example is the use of AI for automated content generation. Some companies are already using AI to automatically write articles, product descriptions, and even entire books. This type of AI can also be used to create graphic content such as logos, posters and even animated videos.

Another field of application is image and video editing. AI can be used to automatically enhance images and videos, apply color corrections or remove unwanted elements from the image. Another application is the automated transcription of audio and video content. AI systems can be used to recognize speech and convert it into text, making it easier to create subtitles or transcripts of interviews or podcasts.

AI systems can also help design websites and user interfaces. By analyzing user data, AI systems can automatically create personalized designs based on the user's preferences and interests. The analysis of user behavior can also be used to make predictions about user behavior and thus create a better user experience.

Another area where AI can be used is in the analysis of social media data. AI systems can be used to analyze users' social media activity to gain insights into trends and preferences. Businesses can use this data to improve their marketing strategies and develop targeted campaigns.

The application of AI in media design offers numerous advantages. On the one hand, AI systems can increase productivity and save time because they can automate certain tasks. On the other hand, AI systems can improve the quality of content by automatically performing optimizations or creating personalized designs. Another advantage is that AI systems can analyze data and gain insights that would be difficult for humans to see alone.

However, it is important to note that AI systems are not perfect and that human creativity and expertise are still essential. However, AI can support and improve the creative process by automating repetitive tasks and providing new insights.

There are other applications of AI in media design. An example is the use of Generative Adversarial Networks (GANs) to automatically generate images and graphics. GANs consist of two neural networks competing: a generator that creates images and a discriminator that decides whether an image was created by the generator or by a real human.

This technology can be used in advertising and marketing to generate visually appealing content. Companies can use it to quickly and cost-effectively create images and graphics that are specifically tailored to their target audience. Another advantage is that the images can be adjusted in real time to reflect changes in the target audience or in the market.

Another example is the use of AI-based recommendation systems. These systems analyze user behavior and recommend content based on the user's interests. This is already being used by many streaming services like Netflix and Amazon Prime Video to give their customers personalized recommendations.

There are also applications of AI in the music industry. Some artists use AI-based tools to generate melodies and rhythms, which are then used in their songs. Others use AI-based technologies to tailor their music to different audiences and platforms.

3.11) Security

AI-based systems can help improve the efficiency, accuracy, and speed of security measures and minimize the impact of errors or human error.

An example of the application of AI in the security industry is video surveillance. AI-based systems can use machine learning algorithms to learn to recognize suspicious behavior and automatically trigger alarms when certain criteria are met. This technology can help reduce security incident response times and increase the efficiency of security personnel.

Another example of the application of AI in the security industry is predicting security risks. AI-based systems can analyze large amounts of data to identify patterns and trends related to security risks. This information can then be used to take preventive action and mitigate potential threats.

In addition, AI can also be used in biometric identification. AI-based systems can recognize and identify faces, voices, fingerprints, and other biometric data. This can help prevent unauthorized access to secure premises and ensure only authorized individuals have access to sensitive information or assets.

Another application of AI in the security industry is process automation. AI-based systems can automate repetitive tasks such as checking safety equipment, maintaining safety devices, or monitoring entrances and exits. This saves costs and minimizes human error.

However, there are also challenges in applying AI in the security industry. One challenge is that AI-based systems are only as good as the data they use. If the data is erroneous or insufficient, this can lead to errors in the predictions or detections. Another challenge is that AI-based systems are unable to replicate human judgment or emotional intelligence.

Overall, the application of AI in the security industry offers many advantages, such as higher efficiency, better accuracy and faster response times to security incidents. However, it is important that technology is used carefully and does not completely replace human judgment and experience.

3.12) <u>Entertainment Industry</u>

AI-based systems have diverse applications in the industry, ranging from personalizing content and optimizing sales strategies to creating new, innovative formats.

One of the most important applications of AI in the entertainment industry is content personalization. AI-based algorithms can analyze large amounts of data to understand consumer behavior and preferences. This information can then be used to generate personalized recommendations for movies, music, books, and other content. This not only improves the customer experience, but also improves customer loyalty.

Another application of AI in the entertainment industry is the optimization of sales strategies. AI-based systems can use data analysis to identify trends and patterns in consumer behavior and use this as a basis to make better marketing and sales strategy decisions. This can help increase the effectiveness of advertising campaigns and increase the profitability of distribution channels.

Another important area where AI has applications in entertainment is creative production. For example, AI-based systems can help generate soundtracks and sound effects or automatically create clips by analyzing existing footage. This can help reduce the workload for creative teams and increase efficiency in content production.

Otherwise, AI also makes it possible to create new formats and experiences in the entertainment industry. For example, virtual reality or augmented reality experiences can be developed that are tailored to consumers' individual preferences and interests. AI-based systems can also help create new business models in the industry, for example by developing personalized streaming platforms or creating interactive experiences.

However, there are also challenges in applying AI in the entertainment industry. One challenge is that creativity and human empathy cannot be fully replicated by AI systems. Another challenge is that AI-based systems are only as good as the data they use. If the data is erroneous or insufficient, this may lead to errors in the recommendations or forecasts.

3.13 <u>Sports</u>

Artificial Intelligence (AI) has impacted many areas of our lives, and sport is no exception. In fact, applying AI to sports has brought some notable benefits that can improve both athlete performance and analytics.

1. Using AI technologies such as machine learning and computer vision allows coaches and athletes to gather and analyze vital information to drive performance improvements. Here are some of the ways AI is already being used in esports:

2. Injury Prediction and Prevention: AI can help prevent injuries in athletes by recognizing patterns in training and game activities that can lead to injuries. Training plans can then be adjusted to minimize injuries.

3. Performance Analysis: AI can help coaches collect and analyze performance data from athletes to identify strengths and weaknesses. This can help identify specific areas where athletes can improve their performance.

4. Game Strategies: AI can also help develop and adjust game strategies by collecting and analyzing data on team and player performance. This allows tactical adjustments to be made to increase success on the pitch.

5. Training Optimization: AI can also help optimize training plans for athletes by collecting and analyzing data about their physical performance and progress. In this way, training programs can be more specifically tailored to the individual needs of the athletes.

6. Referee Support: AI can also help support referees and on-field decision-making by analyzing real-time data and video footage to enable better decision-making.

Overall, the application of AI in sports offers many advantages for athletes and coaches. Analyzing data and spotting patterns can help drive performance improvements and prevent injuries. As AI technology continues to evolve, its impact on sport will only continue to grow.

(4)

HUMAN RESPONSIBILITY IN THE ERA OF ARTIFICIAL INTELLIGENCE:
A Discussion on Challenges and Solutions

"Artificial intelligence will not rule the world, but it will change our lives." - Kai-Fu Lee, CEO of Sinovation Ventures

Artificial intelligence (AI) has made tremendous strides recently and is being used increasingly in areas ranging from automating workflows to developing new drugs. While the benefits and opportunities of AI are obvious, we also need to recognize the risks and challenges that come with using it. The rapid development of AI technologies has raised many questions, especially in relation to ethical and social aspects, such as the automation of workplaces, the privacy issues and the potential impact on humanity. In this chapter we will look at the risks and challenges of AI and examine the possible consequences to get a better understanding of how we can use this technology responsibly.

4.1 The ethical implications of AI: responsible use and challenges

Artificial intelligence (AI) has the potential to change our world and improve our lives in many areas. From the automation of workflows to the development of new drugs, AI has already found applications in many areas. However, there are also concerns about the ethical implications and biases that come with using AI.

One of the biggest problems with using AI is that it's only as intelligent as the data it's based on. If the data is biased or biased, the AI will be biased accordingly. For example, an AI trained on historical data to select applicants for a job might have unconscious biases towards certain groups that have experienced discrimination in the past.

Another problem with using AI is the issue of accountability. Who is responsible if an AI makes wrong decisions or acts discriminatory? Should the developer of the AI be held accountable, or should the responsibility be shifted to the user or the AI owner? These questions are difficult to answer and will likely lead to litigation if not addressed early.

Another issue with using AI is the issue of privacy. AI systems typically collect large amounts of data about users to improve their ability to make decisions. But what happens to this data and who has access to it? There is a risk that this data could be misused by third parties or used for unethical purposes.

To address these ethical concerns and biases, it is important that AI developers and users are aware of these issues and ensure their systems are as fair and transparent as possible. One way to achieve this is to carefully monitor the data used for AI decision-making and ensure that it is not biased or biased. It is also important to define clear responsibilities for AI decision-making and ensure user privacy is protected.

Overall, the use of AI must be done with care and responsibility to ensure it is used in a way that is consistent with the values and principles of our society. We need to be aware that using AI can raise ethical concerns and biases and that it is important to address these issues early on to ensure that AI improves our lives in a positive and ethical way.

4.2 <u>Automation and its consequences for the world of work</u>

From automating production processes to developing self-driving cars, AI is everywhere. However, increasing automation also brings risks, particularly in relation to job losses.

Concerns about job losses due to the use of AI are not unfounded. In fact, there are already examples showing that AI can perform certain tasks faster, more efficiently and at lower cost than human workers. For example, AI systems in the manufacturing industry can take over repetitive tasks such as assembly work or quality control. In the area of customer care, too, chatbots and virtual assistants can already solve certain customer questions and problems.

This development means that more and more people are afraid of losing their jobs. In particular, simple activities that can easily be automated are affected by this development. But even skilled workers are not protected from the risk of losing their job due to AI. Professions like lawyers, accountants or even doctors could be replaced by AI in some aspects of their work.

To counteract these risks, we must be aware that AI is not only a technological advance, but also a societal challenge. We must ensure that we harness the benefits of AI to improve our quality of life and the competitiveness of our businesses, but we must also ensure that we mitigate the negative impact of AI on jobs and working conditions.

One way to do this is to ensure we prepare our workforce for the demands of the new world of work. We need to invest in the education and upskilling of workers to ensure they have the skills needed to thrive in the AI-based economy. In addition, we also need to ensure that we have a social network that offers support to those who lose their jobs due to AI implementations.

Overall, it is important that we are aware that the use of AI is not without risks. But rather than resisting automation, let's focus on building a future where AI helps improve the quality of our lives while ensuring no one is left behind.

4.3 AI and the challenges for information security

In particular, privacy and security pose a major risk as AI collects and processes large amounts of personal data.

Collecting data is an essential part of AI. Machines have to analyze large amounts of data to train models and ultimately make decisions independently. However, this also means that companies and organizations that use AI collect an enormous amount of personal data. This data can be stolen by hackers or misused by the companies themselves to violate people's privacy.

Another problem is that AI-based systems are also vulnerable to manipulation and misuse. Attackers can try to disrupt the system by introducing misinformation or malicious data, for example to make wrong decisions or to discriminate against certain people. There is also a risk that AI systems will develop biases that influence decision-making due to biases in the data.

To counteract these risks, companies, and organizations that use AI must take appropriate security precautions and data protection measures. This includes, for example, ensuring that personal data is only used for the purpose for which it was collected. Furthermore, It is important that data is encrypted and stored on secure servers to prevent unauthorized access.

In addition, AI-based systems should be tested regularly to ensure they are working correctly and have no security vulnerabilities. A check for bias and bias in the data is also required to ensure that the system's decisions are fair and non-discriminatory.

Overall, it is important that companies and organizations using AI are aware that privacy and security pose major risks. They must ensure that appropriate measures are in place to protect people's privacy and ensure that the decisions AI-based systems make are fair and objective.

4.4 The Limits of AI at War: Where Technology Meets Human Intuition

The application of artificial intelligence (AI) in war has become increasingly important lately. From autonomous drones to self-driving vehicles, there are a variety of applications that enable militaries to be more effective and efficient. While some experts argue that AI can offer many advantages in war, there are also concerns about its ethical and moral implications.

One of the most obvious uses of AI in war is the use of autonomous drones. These drones can operate without human control, identifying and attacking targets. An example of this is the Predator drone used by the US during the war in Afghanistan. The drone was used to conduct airstrikes and perform targeted kills.

Another example of the application of AI in war is the use of self-driving vehicles. These vehicles can be used to perform logistical tasks, such as delivering supplies to troops. They can also be used to scout enemy territory and gather intel without endangering human soldiers.

Another example of the application of AI in war is the use of intelligent weapon systems. These systems can autonomously identify and engage targets without human intervention. An example of this is the Russian S-400 anti-missile system, which is capable of automatically tracking and shooting down targets.

Although AI can offer many benefits in warfare, there are also concerns about its ethical and moral implications. One of the biggest concerns is the possibility that autonomous systems can affect human life without human supervision and control. There is also a possibility that autonomous systems could be faulty and attack innocent civilians.

Another issue is accountability for decisions made by autonomous systems. If an autonomous system makes a mistake or makes an incorrect decision, who is responsible for it? Should the manufacturer of the system, the operator, or the system itself be held responsible?

Overall, there are both pros and cons to using AI in war. It is important that governments and militaries carefully consider the ethical and moral implications before deploying autonomous systems. It is also important that the development of AI in war is transparent and that there are clear rules and guidelines in place to ensure autonomous systems are used responsibly.

4.5 The AI debate: where AI reaches its limits

Artificial intelligence (AI) is a ubiquitous topic these days and has found its way into many areas of our lives. From automatic speech recognition to face recognition, AI is used in various applications. Nevertheless, there are also many things that AI cannot do. In this article, we'll take a closer look at some of these limitations.

1. AI cannot replace human intuition is an important part of the human thought process and refers to the ability to make quick decisions using experience and gut feeling. Although AI can analyze large amounts of data and recognize patterns, it cannot replace human intuition. People are capable of making decisions based not solely on data or facts, but on empathy, experience, and personal background.

2. AI can't make moral decisions AI can make decisions based on rules, but it can't make moral decisions. Moral decisions require an understanding of ethical principles and an assessment of consequences and risks. While AI can be programmed to make moral decisions, it has no moral consciousness or intuition. It cannot understand what is morally right or wrong without being taught those rules by humans.

3. AI Cannot Understand Human Emotions are very complex and diverse, encompassing a variety of factors such as empathy, intuition, love, and compassion. AI has no emotions or understanding of them. Although AI is capable of recognizing and responding to human emotions, it lacks the ability to truly understand and respond to those emotions.

4. AI cannot replace creativity is an important part of human thinking and refers to the ability to develop and generate new ideas. While AI can make decisions based on rules and patterns, it lacks the ability to come up with new ideas or be creative. Although AI can recognize existing patterns, it cannot recognize new patterns or generate new creative solutions.

5. AI Cannot Build Personal Relationships are an important part of our lives and relate to the ability to interact with other people on an emotional level. Although AI can simulate human interactions, it cannot create personal relationships. AI has no emotional intelligence or empathy and cannot truly interact with others on a human level.

In summary, AI has many limitations and is unable to replace human skills such as intuition, empathy, creativity and moral understanding. Although AI can analyze large amounts of data and make decisions based on rules, it cannot make decisions based on human experience, emotions and moral values.

It is important to emphasize that AI should not be viewed as a replacement for human intelligence. Instead, AI can be used to complement human intelligence. By combining AI and human intelligence, we can solve complex problems faster and more efficiently and make better decisions.

In addition, we must be aware of the potential dangers associated with the use of AI. One of the biggest concerns is the possibility of AI-based systems spiraling out of control and producing unexpected or undesirable results. It is therefore important that we ensure that we have full control over AI-based systems and that they are used in an ethical manner.

Overall, AI is a powerful tool that can help us in many areas. However, it has its limitations and should not be viewed as a substitute for human intelligence. It is important that we are aware of these limitations and ensure that we are using AI in a responsible and ethical manner.

4.6 AI: An opportunity for business and society

Artificial intelligence (AI) has made enormous progress in recent years and will play an increasingly important role in the future. It is therefore important that both individuals and companies prepare for a future with AI. This article shares some tips on how to prepare for a future with AI.

FOR PRIVATE INDIVIDUALS

1. Learn more about AI: It is important that individuals understand what AI is and how it works. There are many online courses and books that can help learn more about AI. This includes free resources like YouTube videos or podcasts. If you want to delve deeper into the subject, you can also take a course at a university or technical college.

2. Follow the developments: It is important that private individuals follow the developments in the field of AI in order to understand what new opportunities are emerging. Blogs and trade journals can be used for this. Social media platforms such as Twitter or LinkedIn also offer opportunities to keep up to date with the latest developments.

3. Use AI-based applications: There are many AI-based applications that are already available today. For example, a language assistant like Siri or Alexa can help simplify everyday life. AI systems are also used in e-commerce to provide personalized recommendations or to optimize the shopping experience.

4. Think about the ethical issues: It is important for individuals to think about the ethical issues surrounding AI. For example, they should consider whether they are willing to share personal data to use AI-based services. It is important that this decision is made consciously and not out of ignorance or convenience.

5. Develop your own projects: If you want to deal more intensively with AI, you can develop your own projects. There are many open-source platforms and frameworks that help to develop your own AI applications. Again, online courses and communities can help to get support and feedback.

FOR COMPANIES

1. Identify areas of application: Companies should consider in which areas AI can be used to improve their processes. For example, AI can help optimize production or improve customer care. For this purpose, the company's own processes should be analyzed and potential for optimization identified.

2. Invest in training your employees: It is important that employees have the skills to use AI-based applications. Companies should therefore invest in the training of their employees. Training, workshops or the offer of online courses can be used for this.

3. Make sure your data is well-structured: AI needs large amounts of data to work. Businesses should ensure their data is well-structured and organized for use by AI systems. Data management tools or AI-based solutions can be used for this to organize and structure data.

4. Experiment with AI-based solutions: Organizations should experiment and try out AI-based solutions to see what the possibilities are. External service providers or start-ups specializing in the development of AI solutions can also be used for this. Here, too, it is important to analyze your processes and search specifically for areas of application.

5. Think about the impact on employees: Organizations should also think about the impact on their employees. AI can automate or improve certain activities, which

can have an impact on the employment situation. It is important that companies prepare for these changes and, if necessary, take measures to support their employees.

In summary, it is important that both individuals and companies prepare for a future with AI. This can be done by learning about AI, following developments, using AI-based applications, developing your own projects, identifying areas of application, investing in employee training, structuring the data, experimenting with AI-based Solutions and thinking about the impact on employees are made. Anyone who deals with the topic of AI at an early stage can benefit from the many opportunities that will arise in the future.

CHANCES OF AI IN THE FREE ECONOMY

Artificial intelligence (AI) has gained increasing importance in business recently. The application of AI offers companies many opportunities to become more efficient and competitive. This article lists some key opportunities presented by AI applications in business.

1. *Automation of workflows*

One of the greatest opportunities of AI applications is the automation of workflows. AI systems can take over repetitive and time-consuming tasks that are normally performed by human workers. This allows companies to save time and resources and increase productivity.

2. *Optimization of business processes*

AI systems can optimize business processes, for example, by automatically analyzing data and providing insights. By analyzing data, companies can make decisions faster and more accurately, increasing their efficiency and profitability.

3. *Personalization of customer interactions*

AI systems can also be used to enhance the personalization of customer interactions. By analyzing customer data, companies can provide personalized offers and recommendations to increase customer retention and satisfaction.

4. *Improvement of product designs*

AI applications can also help improve product designs by analyzing data to identify trends and customer preferences. In this way, companies can develop products that better meet customer needs, thereby increasing their competitiveness.

5. *Prediction of future trends*

By analyzing large amounts of data, AI systems can also be used to predict future trends. In this way, companies can react more quickly to changes in the market and adapt their products and services accordingly to remain competitive.

Overall, the application of AI in business offers many opportunities to become more efficient, productive and competitive. Companies that integrate AI systems into their workflows can increase their efficiency and profitability, and thus be successful in the long term. However, it is important to note that AI applications are not without risks and require careful planning and implementation to ensure they are used effectively and safely.

OPPORTUNITIES OF AI IN MEDICINE

Artificial intelligence (AI) offers many opportunities for medical practice. AI applications can help make diagnoses faster and more accurate, improve the treatment of diseases and support research. This article lists some key opportunities of AI applications in medicine.

1. *Earlier diagnosis of diseases*

AI systems can be used to diagnose diseases faster and more accurately. By analyzing medical images such as X-rays or CT scans, AI systems can detect abnormalities that human eyes may miss. In this way, diagnoses can be made earlier, which can improve treatment chances and cure rates.

2. *Personalized treatment*

AI systems can also help develop personalized treatment options. By analyzing patient data such as genetic information or medical records, AI systems can develop more accurate and effective treatment plans tailored to the patient's individual needs.

3. *Improving medical imaging*

AI systems can also improve medical imaging. By analyzing medical images, AI systems can identify and flag abnormalities to help doctors diagnose. They can also help improve image quality by automatically correcting images and making them less noisy.

4. *Research and development support*

AI systems can also help in the research and development of new treatment options. By analyzing large amounts of data, AI systems can identify connections between diseases and genes or environmental factors. These findings can then be used to develop new treatment options or improve existing treatments.

5. *Reduction of errors*

AI systems can also help reduce errors in medical practice. By automating tasks like managing patient records or prescribing medication, human error can be minimized. AI systems can also help prevent medical emergencies by monitoring vital signs or warning of impending complications.

OPPORTUNITIES OF AI IN THE EDUCATION SECTOR

AI systems can help improve the educational experience, personalize learning processes and increase the effectiveness of educational programs. This article lists some top opportunities of AI applications in education.

1. _Personalized learning processes_

AI systems can help to personalize the learning process. By analyzing data such as study behavior, interests and skills, AI systems can create personalized learning plans tailored to the needs of each student. This can help make the learning process more effective and efficient, as students can absorb the information in their own way and at their pace.

2. _Automation of tasks_

AI systems can also help automate tasks in education. For example, AI systems can be used to automatically grade tests and assignments and provide feedback. This can help reduce the workload for teachers while ensuring that assessments are fair and objective.

3. _Improving access to education_

AI systems can also help improve access to education. By providing online learning materials, students can access educational resources regardless of their location. AI systems can also help reduce educational barriers for students with learning disabilities by providing personalized learning processes and special adjustments.

4. _Improving the quality of teaching_

AI systems can also help improve teaching quality. By analyzing classroom performance, AI systems can provide teachers with feedback and recommendations to improve their teaching methods. AI systems can also help optimize curricula to ensure they are aligned with student needs.

5. _Improving educational research_

AI systems can also help improve educational research. By analyzing large amounts of data, AI systems can identify connections between learning methods, student performance and other factors. These insights can then be used to optimize educational programs and make them more effective.

OPPORTUNITIES OF AI IN ENVIRONMENTAL PROTECTION

By analyzing large amounts of data, AI systems can help to identify, predict and solve environmental problems. This article lists some key opportunities presented by AI applications in environmental protection.

1. *Detection of environmental problems*

AI systems can help identify and monitor environmental problems. For example, AI systems can be used to analyze satellite data and identify pollution. AI systems can also be used to analyze air quality data and predict the spread of air pollution. These insights can help to take quick and effective action to combat environmental problems.

2. *Precision farming*

AI systems can also be used in farming to optimize resource consumption and maximize production. For example, AI systems can be used to analyze soil conditions and weather to determine the optimal time for sowing and harvesting. AI systems can also help optimize the use of fertilizers and pesticides to minimize environmental impact.

3. *Natural reserve*

AI systems can also help improve conservation. For example, AI systems can be used to monitor wildlife movement and identify threats such as poaching or habitat loss. AI systems can also be used to identify and combat invasive species to conserve biodiversity.

4. _Sustainable energy production_

AI systems can also help improve the sustainability of energy production. For example, AI systems can be used to analyze the energy needs of buildings and suggest optimization measures to reduce energy consumption. AI systems can also be used to optimize energy production from renewable sources such as solar or wind power to maximize efficiency and minimize environmental impact.

5. _Prediction of natural disasters_

AI systems can also help predict and minimize natural disasters. For example, AI systems can be used to analyze weather data and predict the occurrence of natural disasters such as storms or floods. AI systems can also be used to monitor earthquakes and volcanoes to minimize the risk of disasters.

4.7 <u>Critical Analysis of AI from an Ethical & Societal Perspective</u>

From voice assistants to autonomous vehicles, AI has the potential to make our lives easier, more efficient, and safer. However, there is also a growing concern that AI systems can also have negative impacts. Therefore, a critical analysis of AI is essential to ensure that its development and use is ethical and responsible.

One of the most important reasons for a critical analysis of AI is the possibility to discover and correct unintentional or even conscious biases in AI systems. AI systems are based on data, and when that data is incomplete or inaccurate, it can contain bias and bias. These biases can lead AI systems to make decisions based on discrimination or bias, which can have negative effects, particularly for certain populations. A critical analysis of AI systems can help identify and correct these biases.

Another important reason for a critical analysis of AI systems is the ability to understand their impact on jobs and the labor market. Some studies suggest that AI systems can perform certain tasks faster and more efficiently than humans, which could lead to job losses. However, it is also possible that AI systems can create new jobs and support human workers. A critical analysis of AI systems can help to better understand the impact on the labor market and make policy decisions to ensure that nobody is disadvantaged by technological advances.

Another important aspect when critically analyzing AI systems is their transparency and accountability. AI systems can be difficult to understand due to their complexity, making it difficult to explain their decisions or take responsibility. A critical analysis of AI systems can help develop standards and protocols that ensure AI systems are transparent and that their decisions are made responsibly.

In conclusion, a critical analysis of AI systems is essential to ensure that their development and application is done responsibly and ethically. Such an analysis can help identify and correct biases and biases, better understand the impact on the labor market, and improve the transparency and accountability of AI systems. It is important that society critically question the development of AI. Although AI systems have the potential to make our lives easier, more efficient and safer, there are also concerns that they can diminish human dignity and autonomy and contribute to the reinforcement of prejudice and discrimination. AI developers have a responsibility to consider ethical implications to ensure that AI systems are developed and deployed in accordance with human well-being values and principles.

. AI regulation and governance is essential to ensure that the development and use of AI is in line with our values and principles.

The government plays an important role in regulating AI. She is responsible for ensuring that AI systems are developed and deployed in accordance with societal values and principles. AI regulation should aim to ensure user safety and privacy, prevent discrimination and promote transparency. In addition, the regulation of AI systems should ensure that they are ethically responsible and human-centric.

One way to regulate AI is to develop standards and certification processes that ensure AI systems meet specific requirements. Governments can also incentivize companies that develop and promote ethical AI systems to ensure they meet their responsibilities. Governments should also be able to impose sanctions on companies that violate ethical standards.

International cooperation is also important to ensure effective regulation and governance of AI. Since AI is a global phenomenon, governments and organizations should work together internationally to develop standards and regulations that can be recognized and implemented worldwide. International cooperation can also help ensure that AI systems are not used to invade other countries or carry out illegal activities.

It is also important that the regulation of AI is flexible and adaptable as the technology continues to evolve. Regulations should be regularly reviewed and updated to ensure they reflect the latest developments in technology.

Overall, AI regulation and governance is critical to ensure AI systems are developed and deployed in line with our values and principles. Governments play an important role in developing and enforcing regulations, while international cooperation can ensure that these standards are recognized and implemented around the world. It is important that regulation of AI is flexible and adaptable to ensure it stays in line with the latest developments in technology

4.8 Recommendations for the responsible use of AI systems in everyday life

The use of artificial intelligence (AI) in everyday life is no longer a dream of the future. More and more companies are turning to AI technologies to optimize their business and better serve their customers. But there are now numerous ways for private individuals to integrate AI into their everyday lives and to benefit from the advantages of this technology. This article shows some ways in which private individuals can use AI in everyday life.

1. Virtual Assistants Some of the most popular virtual assistants are Apple's Siri, Google Assistant and Amazon's Alexa. These AI-supported language assistants help to organize everyday life by setting reminders, creating shopping lists or arranging appointments.

2. Personalized recommendations AI systems can make personalized recommendations based on user data. This is particularly useful in areas such as music, film and TV, but also in online shopping platforms or news apps.

3. Smart home systems AI systems can also be used to control a smart home. By connecting to smart devices such as light switches, thermostats or door locks, you can automate your home and thus save time and energy.

4. Medical applications AI systems can also be used in the healthcare sector. An example is the detection of diseases based on symptoms or medical images. But health data such as steps, sleep or heart rate can also be tracked thanks to AI technologies.

5. Creative applications AI systems can also be used to support creative activities. For example, they can help with writing texts or drawing pictures.

However, it is important to also consider the risks and challenges of using AI in everyday life. Data protection and privacy are important factors that should be considered when using AI systems. Users should also make sure that they do not become completely dependent on AI and do not neglect to think and act independently.

Overall, the use of AI in everyday life offers numerous advantages and can make everyday life easier. However, it is important to use this technology responsibly and consciously to meet one's needs while minimizing the risks and challenges.

Ten tips for dealing with AI:

1. Understand how AI works: It is important to understand how AI works to be able to use it better. Read up on basic concepts like machine learning, deep learning, and neural networks.

2. Only use trustworthy AI systems: Make sure that the AI systems you use come from reputable providers who adhere to ethical standards.

3. Be skeptical of automated decisions: Do not blindly rely on automated decisions made by AI systems, but question the results critically and consider them as a clue, not a definitive answer.

4. Respect data protection and privacy: Use AI systems that protect your privacy and keep your data safe.

5. Monitor the AI systems: Keep an eye on the AI systems and regularly check their results. This allows you to identify and resolve potential problems early on.

6. Avoid AI bias: AI systems can have biases based on the data they were trained on. Make sure the data you use is balanced and representative to minimize AI bias.

7. Don't use AI as the sole solution: Use AI systems to support your decisions, but don't solely rely on their results.

8. Keep the costs in mind: AI systems can be expensive, so make sure the benefits outweigh the costs before investing in them.

9. Training and Education: The more you know about AI, the better able you will be to use it. Use free online resources and courses to educate yourself.

10. Be Responsible and Ethical: Always use AI systems in a responsible and ethical manner. Make sure you don't cause discrimination or any other negative impact on people or groups.

These are just a few tips for dealing with AI, but it's important to emphasize that the technology is evolving, bringing with it new challenges and opportunities. Continuous training and attention to changes in the field of AI are therefore essential.

SUMMARY

In this book, we have dealt with various aspects of artificial intelligence (AI). We have looked at their history, development, and application in various fields such as business, medicine, education and environmental protection. We also discussed the ethical implications of AI and stressed the importance of critical analysis.

AI is a technology that enables machines to acquire human-like cognitive abilities such as speech recognition, image processing, and pattern recognition. AI systems are becoming increasingly intelligent and can now perform complex tasks such as self-driving cars, language translation and even medical diagnostics.

We have shown that AI represents an incredible opportunity for humanity to solve complex problems and improve our lives. In business, AI can help increase the efficiency of companies, improve customer loyalty and create new business models. In medicine, AI can help diagnose diseases faster and more accurately, optimize treatments and improve healthcare for patients. In education, AI can help create personalized learning plans for students, streamline lessons, and increase the effectiveness of educational institutions. In environmental protection, AI can help combat climate change, increase energy efficiency and improve the protection of endangered species.

However, there are also concerns about the impact of AI on society and our lives. One of the biggest concerns is the impact of AI on human dignity and autonomy. As machines become more intelligent and make human-like decisions, there is a risk that human autonomy will be limited. There is also concern that human dignity could be compromised through the use of AI systems.

Another problem is the potential of AI to reinforce prejudice and discrimination. When AI systems perpetuate discrimination based on bias in the data they were trained on, it can have serious consequences for society. For example, this can result in minorities or disadvantaged groups being further disadvantaged.

It is therefore important that we are aware of these concerns and ensure that AI is developed and used in line with our values and principles. We must ensure that AI systems are safe, ethical, and human-centric. This requires a critical analysis of AI and its impact on society.

Appropriate regulation and governance of AI is crucial to ensure AI systems are secure and trustworthy. The government plays an important role in this by creating regulatory frameworks that encourage the development and use of AI systems in line with our values and principles. This regulation should aim to make AI systems transparent and accountable, to ensure that decisions can be understood and verified by machines.

Another important component in the regulation of AI is international cooperation. AI is a global technology being developed and deployed in different countries and regions around the world. Cooperation between countries and regions is necessary to ensure that AI systems are ethical and safe, wherever they are developed and deployed.

Finally, it is important that AI developers and users recognize their responsibility to consider ethical implications when developing and using AI systems. We should ensure that AI systems are human-centric and designed to enhance human life, rather than detract from it. The development of AI systems should be transparent to ensure that the decisions made by machines can be understood and verified.

Overall, AI offers tremendous potential to improve our lives and solve complex problems. However, we must ensure that we address the concerns surrounding AI and ensure that the development and use of AI systems is consistent with our values and principles. Only then can we ensure that AI helps create a better future for all of us.

EPILOGUE

Hey,

I hope you enjoyed the book about AI and learned a lot! Since you seem genuinely interested in the topic, I wanted to recommend another free work that you can use to learn how to make money using AI.

There are many ways that AI can be used to generate income, whether it's through the development of AI-based products and services or the use of AI in marketing and sales strategies. The free work that I would like to recommend to you is a book called: "The AI Bible, Making Money with Artificial Intelligence: Real Case Studies and How-To's".

This e-book will give you a comprehensive look at the different ways AI can be used to generate income. It contains practical tips and examples that will help you develop and implement your own ideas. It also provides a step-by-step guide to creating your own AI project.

I think this free work is a great addition to the book you have just read. It gives you practical guidance on how to apply what you have learned and reap the benefits of AI.

"The AI Bible, earning money with artificial intelligence: Real case studies and instructions for implementation."

Good luck and success in your future AI projects!

GLOSSARY

1. Artificial Intelligence (AI): A term that refers to systems and technologies that can simulate human-like intelligence and abilities.

2. Machine Learning (ML): A branch of AI that focuses on algorithms and models that enable a system to learn from data and make predictions.

3. Neural Networks: A pattern recognition approach inspired by biological neural networks and widely used in image and speech recognition.

4. Deep Learning: A specialized neural network approach that uses multiple layers of neurons to solve complex problems.

5. Natural Language Processing (NLP): An AI technology that enables computers to understand, interpret, and generate human language.

6. Computer Vision: An area of AI that focuses on the ability of machines to process, interpret, and understand visual information.

7. Big Data: A collection of data that is so large or complex that it cannot be processed using traditional data processing techniques.

8. Algorithm: A sequence of instructions executed by a computer to accomplish a specific task.

9. Data Analysis: The process of examining and interpreting data to identify insights and patterns.

10.   Bias: A systematic error in the data or in an AI model that can lead to inaccurate results.

www.ingramcontent.com/pod-product-compliance
Lightning Source LLC
Chambersburg PA
CBHW031416160726
47993CB00003B/1259